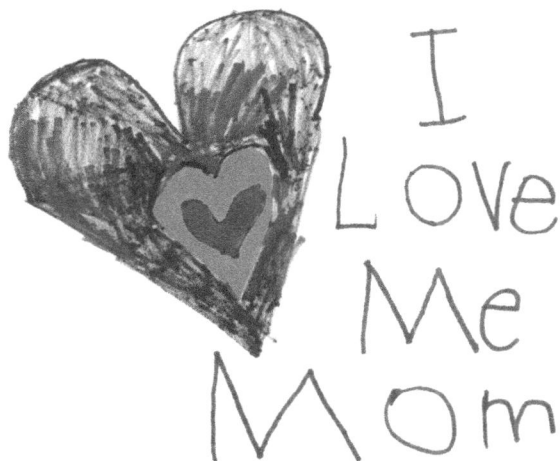

A Guilt-Free Guide to Honoring Yourself

and Empowering Your Kids

I0134492

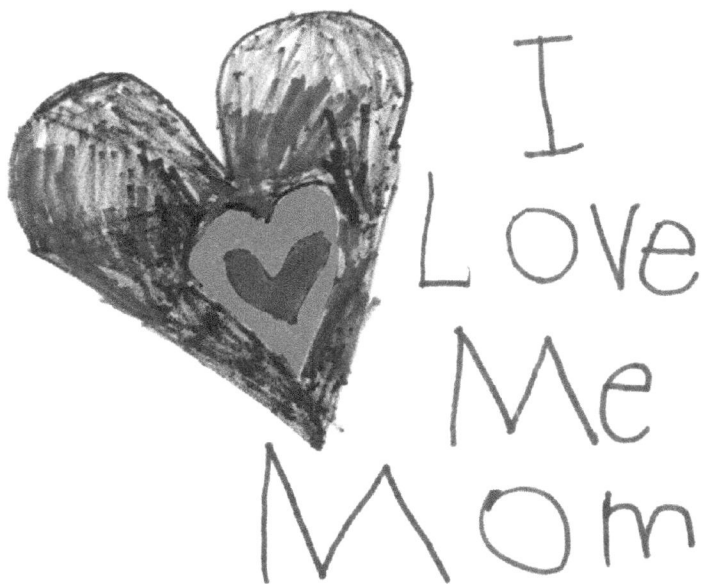

I Love Me Mom

A Guilt-Free Guide to Honoring Yourself

and Empowering Your Kids

Jill Baake

MAVEN
MARK
BOOKS

Published by:
MavenMark Books
A division of HenschelHAUS Books, Inc.
6450 W. Forest Home Ave. Suite 102
Milwaukee, WI 53220
www.HenschelHAUSbooks.com

Please contact the publisher with inquiries about quantity
discounts.

ISBN: 978-159598-109-7

Library of Congress Number and Cataloging-in-Publication Data:
Available on request

Printed in the United States of America.

To Nathan and Rylan—may your lives be filled with love, miracles, and dreams come true.

I AM
special.
And
So Are you.

Acknowledgements

I want to sincerely thank my mom and dad, Diane and Mark Roth, for their unwavering trust and support of my adventures. Who knew what a wild ride life with me would be?!

Thank you to everyone who has provided love and encouragement over the last four years. I love you all, and I feel so blessed to share my life with you. Thank you for believing in me and recognizing my gifts during a time of challenging uncertainty. Special thanks to Michelle Pape and Amy Morgan—you totally rock!

I also want to thank my uncle, Bill Lueders, for being a talented and passionate writer; you helped me to believe that perhaps I also possess some of that writer's DNA.

Thank you to Ryan Peterson for suggesting over and over again that I should write a book. I appreciate your persistence and encouragement. Thank you to Sue Cook, Amy Siewert, my mom (again), and Kira Henschel for your editing expertise.

Thank you to Patty Jackson, my dear friend and mentor. You helped me find my wings and I'm forever grateful.

And thank you to my beautiful children, Nathan and Rylan, for teaching me about love, authenticity, inspira-tion, and perfection. It is an absolute honor to be your mom and I love you more than I could ever express.

—Jill Baake
Hales Corners, Wisconsin
2011

Table of Contents

I
Love
Me
Mom

I Love me.

Introduction

When my son, Nathan, was born, I remember thinking that there should be another word for the love of a child. "Love" just wasn't a strong enough term to describe the feelings that I was experiencing. Sure, I loved my family and friends, the first beautiful spring day, chocolate, and lots of other things, but this was different. This was soul-level, breath-disrupting love. It was an emotion I'd never felt before, so how could it be "just" love? It's been a thrill to live recent years carrying that emotion with me. There was that moment of wonder before my daughter, Rylan, was born … would I feel that same incredible connection with her? What a joy and relief it was when I did!

My experience as a mom has not been what I thought it was going to be. My dream of the "perfect" family with the mom and the dad and the kids and the house and the summer vacations and the happily ever after took a detour when my husband exited our marriage. Our daughter was five months old when he moved out, our son was three. And because sometimes life just needs a major reboot, I left my corporate job two weeks later.

Since Rylan was my second child, I was acutely aware of how fast the first year of life goes by. I'm so thankful for that awareness, because despite the life challenges that I was facing, I made a vow to her. I vowed not to miss her first year of life. I wanted to be completely present and in tune with the wonderment and self-discovery that takes place in that first year. The gift of that vow was that as Rylan was growing and learning and getting to know herself, I was growing and learning and getting to know myself. I was no longer someone's wife or someone's employee; I was just me. She was just her. She served as my daily example of how to live. As the years have gone by, I've continued to grow and learn and expand. The vow that I made to her has been renewed. I now am committed to being present and in tune with the wonder and discovery and unconditional love of me.

My hope is that *I Love Me Mom* will provide you, the mom, an opportunity to begin loving yourself in powerful and joyful ways. In addition, I hope that it allows you to see the value in raising kids who love and appreciate themselves. By living from a place of self-love, our own experiences feel better, and we set an example for our children of love and personal acceptance.

I've received some powerful insights about the roles of parents and kids, and I now work as a Life Coach sharing these ideas with other moms. These insights come from my heart, from my beliefs, and from my experiences. I am so grateful to have learned so much from my kids and from my journey, and I am grateful to have the opportunity to share that learning with you.

Understandings

There are a few things that I've come to believe as truths, and it seems relevant to establish these before jumping in. These ideas are the framework for many of the thoughts in this book. My intention is not to inflict my truth on you, but rather to create a common understanding from which to begin, and allow you the opportunity to see how these truths feel for you.

I believe you love your kids. You want them to grow up to be happy, inspired, well-adjusted, independent, love-filled beings. You work hard to be the best mom you can be, and you take your job as a mom pretty seriously.

I believe that we are spiritual beings. We are literally children of God /Source Energy/the Universe. Within each of us is the DNA of Divinity, in the same way that we each carry the human DNA of our parents. We are the creators of our experience, and there is more to life than what meets the eye. We come into this life with a mission to learn, grow, expand, and love.

At our essence, our core, we are complete love and joy. Any experiences we create outside of love and joy are opportunities to learn and feel, so that we may choose to return to love and joy. I believe children set perfect examples of how easy it is to return to love and joy.

Life is evolutional. We continually grow and change. What we knew to be true yesterday may not be true tomorrow. (Remember how we once believed the earth was flat or that phones had to have wires?) Life has changed considerably over history, and we can trust that it will continue to evolve. I believe that it is changing faster than ever. Our children are part of that rapid progression, and the parenting of decades past no longer meets the needs of our amazing kids.

The only behavior we control is our own. As parents, we often feel it is our responsibility to control our kids and demand appropriate behavior. However, the reality is we can only truly control ourselves. Living by example is the most effective way to influence our kids.

It is fun to be me.

1

A Case for Self-love Parenting

The intention of this chapter is to help you think about love in a new way. We often view love as an external emotion. We love other people, things, or experiences. We don't often examine, however, how our feelings about ourselves affect our day-to-day lives. Our behavior is likely a direct reflection of how we feel about ourselves.

By looking more deeply at the idea of self-love, we can begin to understand the importance of loving who we are and treating ourselves with love and kindness. We readily accept that our kids deserve it, and my hope is that you can also see how much you deserve your own love.

What is Self-love?

Self-love is the core belief that I am enough, capable, lovable, and worthy simply because I am.

Self-love allows me to make decisions and live my life for my best interests, regardless of external circumstances.

Self-love provides the backdrop from which I can create a life of joy and learning.

By lovingly taking care of myself, I empower those around me to do the same with authenticity and joy.

It is critical to understand that self-love does not equate to selfishness. In fact, it is quite the opposite. Selfishness is an act in which one takes from another to meet one's own needs.

Self-love, on the other hand, requires us to take responsibility for our own feelings, our own experiences, and our own desires. We hold complete control of the choices and decisions we make, and we place no blame on others or unforeseen circumstances. There is no taking from anyone else. Self-love is an understanding of our own Divinity and commitment to honoring the precious gift of life.

In addition, self-love is a recognition that we are all capable and perfectly equipped to take care of ourselves. There is no hierarchy of beings—each is enough, capable, lovable, and worthy. I honor that truth within myself, and I honor it in others.

It is not selfish of me to meet my own needs; it *is* selfish of me to require that you meet my needs for me.

It is not selfish of me to trust you to meet your own needs and choose how I consciously meet mine. It is selfish of me to believe that you require me to meet your needs.

In essence, when we come swooping in to meet someone else's needs, we illustrate a belief that others cannot take care of themselves.

For example, I have a need to feel connected. If I am operating from a place of self-love, I ask myself what it is that I need, and then make choices and decisions to meet that need. I might call a friend and make plans to get together. I might Facebook with some people I haven't chatted with for a while. I might go to the gym or the mall to be among group energy. I would make choices in the direction of meeting my need until the need was met.

If I were being selfish, I would look through my phone contacts and feel disappointed by all the friends who never call me. I would whine on Facebook that I'm lonely and life kicks me around, with the intention of making people feel sorry for me and post uplifting comments about how much they love me. It would be up to the outside world to meet my need for connection and, when it failed, I would be extra sad, and use the new information to affirm the idea that I'm not lovable. Instead of sharing joy and love with the community, I would share my disappointment about being let down and my needs would go unmet.

Can you see the difference? When I actively become aware of my own needs and take responsibility for them, I have love and light to share. I consciously create good feelings for myself, and I no longer require others to take care of me.

Critical Role Models

I was in the grocery store with my son Nathan when he was about two years old. He was sitting in the front of the cart, and as we waited in the checkout line, he reached behind him and grabbed a stick of deodorant from the basket, lifted up his arm, and began applying deodorant (with the cap on) under his arms. I enjoyed the entertainment of a toddler pretending to be grown up, and then realized the complexity of what had happened. I had never talked with Nathan about deodorant, nor had I intentionally demonstrated its use. Whoa! This little guy is watching me. He's looking to me to learn how to be "big."

It wasn't about what I was saying; it was about who I was being.

When I think about my children growing into adults, I have many hopes and dreams for them. I want them to be happy, independent, passionate, engaged in life, fun, responsible, self-fulfilled, and so much more. Yet, I've found that moms often feel stressed, overworked, worried, guilty, fearful, unattractive, tired, uninspired, and not good enough. So, if our kids are watching (which they are), what examples are we showing them on how to live their lives?

We learn by example and experience, and we know that parents are the most influential role models in a child's life. This is not news. However, it may be a new perspective for you to realize that how you feel about yourself directly influences how your precious children feel about themselves. If we show our kids that adults are stressed, fearful, and not good enough, they will believe us.

We are critical role models. We serve as the day-to-day examples of how adults behave, communicate, express emotion, and understand the mysteries of life. Yikes! That scary realization can propel us to more fear, anxiety, and pressure about how to parent well. However, the example we set is completely within our control, and there is a very simple focus that can change everything: Self-love.

A mom who has taken the time and energy to fall completely and totally in love with the God-Being she is, lives in a joy and love that not only sets a beautiful example for her children, but also feels powerful, energetic, and capable. Your children have everything they need to walk through this life in joy, authenticity, and love —and so do you.

The following are six concepts to paint a picture of the importance of being a self-love role model.

Peer Pressure

We often think peer pressure begins around school age as a result of our kids wanting to fit in, or as a rite of passage in life. In actuality, peer pressure is modeled at home and taught to kids under the disguise of kindness and caring for others.

Here's an example. The phone rings, and it's the soccer coach. "The snack mom got confused and forgot to get snack for the game. Can you handle the snack responsibilities?" You think, Oh, crap! I have 206 things going on this weekend. I have nothing in the house that can work as a snack for 23 kids. I really wanted to take a shower and have 15 minutes to enjoy my own thoughts this morning.

You instantly do not want to be pinch-hitting snack mom today.

Although your thoughts are clear, you say, "Ummmmm….yeah, I can do that. I wouldn't want to let the kids down." Then, you hang up the phone and get real. You grumble and whine to whoever is within earshot. "Really? Good grief! Now we have to go to the store and spend $15 on snacks for soccer because Mrs. Smith can't get her act together. Get moving, guys, we have to leave right now! I know I said we had some time to hang out, but we have to take care of snack responsibilities for soccer. You want to go to soccer, don't you?" Suddenly, the entire energy of your family has shifted from an enjoyable Saturday morning to an obligated rush filled with grumpiness.

I have bad news, dear well-intentioned mom who is taking one for the team. You have just modeled peer pressure to your precious child. Here is what you demonstrated. When someone asks you to do something, you do it. It doesn't matter if it doesn't feel good or work with your schedule. We make our own needs secondary to the needs of others. The coach needed help, right? Yes, the coach did need help. That does not mean that you need to drop everything and disrupt your entire family's experience to save the day.

So, in a kid-based situation, here's how it might play out. Your son is offered a cigarette from another child. Instantly, he knows that smoking is unhealthy, addictive, and grounds for serious trouble at school and at home. He doesn't really want to smoke. However, he doesn't have the language or the permission to take complete care of himself without concern for the others involved. So, he goes with the thought process he's been shown: "Ummmmm… yeah, I can do that. I wouldn't want to let the kids down."

Let's play the scenario a different way. Coach calls, and instead of agreeing, mom takes a personal inventory and realizes that it is not going to work for her or her family to pick up snacks today. She replies, "Oh, coach, I'm really sorry, but that isn't going to work for us today." Coach is left with the same problem she had before calling, so therefore, she calls the next mom on the list. Next mom answers and says, "Wow, that's so funny, we just picked up snacks and have plenty to bring. No problem, coach."

Children who have witnessed that language and degree of personal responsibility react to the peer situation much differently. They now have the tools and the personal power to take care of their own needs. Upon being offered the cigarette, the child takes a personal inventory, realizes that he really doesn't want to smoke, and responds, "Oh, no, thanks." His choices are now empowered and based on taking care of his own needs, not on meeting the needs of others.

I am not suggesting that you just start saying "no" to everything and removing generosity and empathy from your world. What I am suggesting is that you start putting your needs in the primary position, so that you can give to others from a place of joy and overflow rather than obligation. If the coach had called and you had just bought an extra bag of pretzels and could easily assist with snack duties, then by all means, you step in. You step in because it feels good and doing so does not create a negative situation for you or your family. The point is to start aligning your behavior with what feels good for you. In taking care of your own needs, you demonstrate to your kids that it is okay for them to do the same. Your children already know how to do this. They have an internal compass that regulates self-care. Even an infant has it. When she is hungry, she cries, signifying that she has a need. We have the tools to recognize and meet our needs.

Yet as moms, we sometimes forget that our own needs are of primary importance.

We are born with the capacity for perfect self-care, and as parents, it is wise to allow our kids the opportunities to practice those skills. Your kids will make good decisions to take care of themselves if they have the permission and the communication skills to do so. These communication skills come directly from the powerful modeling you exhibit each day. Model self-love and responsibility, and your children will learn self-love and responsibility.

Perspective

At any given moment, each of us could create a list of the things that are going well in our lives and a list of the things that are going not so well. I believe this is true for every person, regardless of what his or her life looks like from the outside looking in. We all have both the good and the less desirable. The ability to choose our perspective, coupled with the knowledge that "what we focus on expands," produces a powerful tool for understanding and creating our experiences.

What does "what we focus on expands" mean? It means that wherever we invest our thoughts and energy, that area will grow. Like attracts like. What you give is what you receive.

Think of it this way. We all have two gardens. One is filled with beautiful fruits, veggies, and flowers. The other is filled with weeds. We have a finite amount of water and sunlight to nurture our gardens on a daily basis. If we focus the distribution of water on the fruits and veggies, they will thrive and bloom. Likewise, if we water and energize the weed garden, it will flourish and grow.

It's like the bad day scenario. You get out bed and stub your toe. Then you are last in line for the shower at your house, so there's no hot water left. On the way to work, you hit every red light. By lunch time, you've got a pretty good story brewing, so you actively start watching for more bad stuff. Your co-worker burns his popcorn in the microwave, your computer eats the document that you spent all morning working on, and the lady that sits next to you is extra-grumpy and using you as a target.

What we focus on expands. While we're watering the weeds and watching them grow, we continue to create more weed growth.

We have a choice for the distribution of our water and sunlight. We can choose at any given moment whether to focus on the flowers or on the weeds of our lives. When we realize that what we focus on expands, we can actively become more aware of how we distribute our energy and take conscious responsibility to water the good stuff.

This may be different from how you're programmed to deal with life. Many of us, when faced with a bad-feeling situation, go immediately to "fix it" mode. We are going to work on the problem and get to the root of it and change the situation. However, knowing that what we focus on expands, wouldn't putting all our energy into a problem promote the problem to grow? Aren't we then watering the weeds? Oops! We didn't mean to water the weeds, but that's what we've been doing, nonetheless.

The solution is not to ignore the weeds or pretend they don't exist. If you've created a situation in your life that doesn't feel good, I absolutely believe that you should address that situation and move toward creating something better for yourself. You can do this without watering the weeds.

What's great about a thriving garden is that you don't notice the weeds in the same way; you only appreciate the beauty and liveliness of the crop. The process is really quite simple. You notice the weeds and acknowledge them. You then decide what it is that you want to feel, be, or have, and choose to water the wanting with gratitude and love.

I invite you to pay attention to your perspective. If you view your life situations in a negative manner, you attract more negativity. There is always something good you can find to focus on. Always. Even in the worst situation, you can find something to celebrate. September 11, 2001 was one of the most tragic days in U.S. history, yet there was an unparalleled display of kindness among neighbors, generosity of spirit, and unification of people. Even in that literal terror, there was a way to see the positive. And when you can do it on that grand scale, you can certainly do it with day-to-day situations.

Permission

The concept of permission is fascinating. From the moment we can talk, we build up this cycle of asking for permission. At home, it's a constant communication of permissions. "Mom, can I have a snack?" "Mom, can I go outside?" "Mom, can I watch TV?" "Mom, can I go to a friend's house?" "Mom, can I have a puppy?" Then we go to school and we rely on the teacher to grant us permission. When we get into the 'tween and teen years we look to our friends for permission and approval.

For some of us, there is no graduation from the need for approval. If you are in the market for a new car, do you call your dad to get the okay? What about asking your friends if it is okay to make a parenting decision or a relationship choice? We rely on permission and approval throughout our lives. The problem with this process is that, along the way, we lose sight of our ability to make solid, well-serving decisions on our own behalf. We become dependent on others to make our behaviors valid and right. We give away our personal power, and make choices and decisions based on their perspective rather than what we know to be true in our soul.

Inside each of us is a navigation system, an inner voice. It functions perfectly in all situations and will point us in the right direction as Divine beings every time... if we listen. That "right" direction is always for the highest good of ourselves and our lives. When we rely on outside influences for our decisions and choices, we become less and less in tune with our internal navigation system. That little voice inside of us, the one that knows exactly where to go, gets quieter and quieter. We begin to distrust our own knowledge in favor of trusting outside viewpoints. We trust others more than we trust ourselves.

When we put our personal power into the hands of someone else's perception, we become misaligned with our true purpose and mission. We lose our ability to listen to our inner voice, and we come to believe we cannot make good decisions on our own. We become dependent on others and continue to look for permission and approval—all the while becoming more disconnected and miserable inside.

What can you do about it? A lot, actually. As you become aware of your inner voice, you can take steps to actively listen to yourself and trust your inner knowledge. Notice how often you are looking to others for their approval. When you realize that it has happened, stop and check in with yourself. What do you feel you need to do in the situation? What is stopping you from making the decision yourself and trusting that it is absolutely the right call for you?

One of the coolest things about life is that there are very few irreversible decisions. If you decide to buy a new car and it turns out that you don't love the car the way you thought you would, you can sell it! If you think that going to a new restaurant is going to be fun, but you get there and it smells like dirty socks, you can leave! There are few choices that carry such dire consequences that you would require a committee to weigh the options. You know what is right for you. And so do your children.

As conscious adults, we can look at the behavior patterns we have developed, and then start to model a new way of being for our children. The process of learning to trust our inner voice is certainly more involved than the process of nurturing and honoring it throughout our childhood and formative years.

If our kids understood that they had the tools to take perfect care of themselves, they would enter adulthood with the personal power and confidence to conduct their lives in self-honoring and option-filled ways. They hear their inner voices clearly; ours have varying degrees of interference. We would be moving in the right direction to check in with how our kids are feeling about decisions and choices, as opposed to checking in with our parents and peers.

On a day-to-day basis, I encourage you to allow your children to tune into their inner voices. Remembering that few decisions create irrevocable outcomes, when can you let your kids tap into their inner knowledge? When can you communicate that you trust your children's ability to take perfect care of themselves? Offer your children opportunities to think for themselves, and they will become teens and adults who can think for themselves.

You can try responses like, "Wow! I can't wait to see what you decide!" and "I trust you to make the perfect decision for you!" and "What is your heart telling you to do?" These are also great "thought tapes" to play in your head when you're working through a decision for yourself.

As an additional tool, I welcome the opportunity to be your source of permission. The next time you are searching for permission, I hereby grant you the permission to listen to your inner knowing. You are perfectly equipped to make the best decision for you, and the best way to rebuild your communication with your inner voice is to begin using it.

Personal Power

One of the most painful emotions to experience is powerlessness, the feeling that there isn't anything you can do to improve your situation or affect your experience. In actuality, there is no such thing. We always have choices. Always. We have a choice in how we perceive a situation. We have a choice in what action we take next. We have a choice in how we feel about ourselves and those around us. Powerlessness is a complete illusion. Life does not happen to us—we create our experiences.

The experiences we have are a result of the choices we make on a moment-to-moment basis. The choices we make are a result of the thoughts we think. Our thoughts are influenced by such factors as societal norms, childhood and family experiences, personal expectations, religious understandings, and more.

I believe there is a key indicator of whether or not someone will make consistently good choices for herself. That indicator is how she feels about herself and how powerful she feels in her own life. Someone with a good amount of self-love, self-awareness, and knowledge of her own power, is more likely to create experiences filled with love, joy, and connection. That person is making decisions on a moment-to-moment basis from a place of personal power, and would therefore be making decisions that create positive experiences in her life. Consciously, would any of us create pain and suffering if we believed we could create joy and love?

The challenge here is accepting responsibility for your creative power and letting go of being the victim. As you come to realize that you are creating your experiences through your choices, you can then make choices intentionally designed to create whatever it is you would like to experience. However, if you do not take responsibility for what you have already created and appreciate the gifts in those situations, you will likely dismiss your creative power and continue to allow your day-to-day decisions to be based on society, expectations, and luck.

Once you realize that powerlessness is a painful illusion, creating relationships with your children that allow them to feel powerful and in control becomes of massive importance. Although re-learning as an adult is a wonderful process, wouldn't it be even better to learn how powerful you are during childhood?

Your children deserve to hear things like, "You are the boss of you." "You are responsible for your (shoes, toys, homework, etc.)" "I can't wait to see how you figure that out!" "I trust you to know what's best for you." "What are you going to do about that?" "What do you think?" "Wow! Sounds like you're learning something new!" "What do you want to see happen next?"

By allowing your children to understand and work through personal responsibility at a young age, you teach them to exercise their power and listen to their inner voice throughout their childhood. The result? The knowledge, tools, and insights to take care of themselves and operate on behalf of their own best interests. When we love ourselves and know that we deserve joy and happiness, we make decisions that support this belief.

When we are learning something new, it's not uncommon to experience a situation that feels outside of our control and to slide into the victim role. Here's an example.

Recently, a client of mine, Lisa, came to a session to report that she'd had a really great week up until Sunday when it all unraveled. She took me through the series of events. The day was packed with activities. An early pickup of returning in-laws from the airport; lunch with said in-laws with her two children and husband; homework, dinner, a family outing to Disney on Ice, etc. It was early in the day when Lisa began to lose control of her experience. The kids were shouting in the van while she was trying to drive and talk with her back-from-vacation-and-very-excited mother-in-law. Then at the restaurant, she wore the responsibility for taking care of both kids and again entertaining the mother-in-law, because as a good mother, it was her responsibility to do it all (note sarcasm here).

And so it continued...rushing the kids to get where they needed to go, handling all the details, playing hostess, and silently bleeding energy until she got to early evening and was completely spent.

As we chatted about her energy-sucking day, Lisa made a realization. A big one. Lisa realized that there were several times in the day that she knew she was over-extended, but she didn't do anything about it. There were several times in the day that the people around her could have (and would have happily) helped out, pitched in, or stepped up. Lisa realized that she was not a victim of her day. She had created and promoted the crazy, stressful, overwhelming day she suffered. With that realization, Lisa accepted responsibility for her own experience.

What if, instead of being responsible for doing it all, we are only responsible for taking care of our own experience? Not in a selfish, "I won't help you" kind of way, but rather, in an "I take care of me first, and I trust that you will still be taken care of" kind of way.

In the situation above, Lisa realized that she could have asked her husband to quietly entertain the kids in the van. And he would have! She also realized that she could have divided responsibilities at the restaurant. The three other adults there would have happily assisted the children as needed. She realized that she knew she was giving too much, but didn't have the tools (yet) to meet her own needs and allow others to share in the leadership of the family.

Here are some of the tools that Lisa now has for taking care of herself:

- ♦ She is aware of when she is feeling overloaded; awareness is always the first step.
- ♦ She can, in that moment, ask herself, "What is it that I want or need?"
- ♦ She trusts that those around her will respond if she communicates her needs.
- ♦ She is willing to allow others to complete things in their own perfect way—even if their way is different from hers.
- ♦ She knows now that regardless of how the experience goes, she always has choices and personal power to change directions at any time.

We can all choose how we view our experiences and ourselves. Lisa has decided that she is no longer willing to play the victim in her own life. She's taken responsibility for herself, and she has the power to create fun, joyful, remember-when experiences.

Reciprocal Responsibility

We are very often afraid to make changes and take full responsibility for our own experiences because of the effect we think the new behavior will have on the people around us. We believe that if we invest the time and energy into meeting our own needs, then others' needs will go unmet. In reality, whether or not others' needs are met is completely up to them.

We also fear that if we stop giving all our energy to others, we will no longer be seen as lovable or needed. In the journey to self-love, we begin to truly rely on ourselves for evidence of our worthiness and Divinity. We let go of the need for external approval and acknowledgment. If in taking care of and responsibility for myself, I create a dynamic in which you no longer love me, that is an indication of our unbalanced previous relationship. My new behavior is therefore a gift to both of us.

It might be best to look at this concept through an example. Imagine that you are 23 years old and return to live with your mom and dad after college. And your mom does all of your laundry. Every morning, your shirts and pants are in your closet, your socks folded neatly in your drawer, clean linens on your bed, and a towel awaiting your shower. Ahhhhhh. If this was your reality, you likely wouldn't think, "Gee, I should be taking personal responsibility for my laundry. It seems out of balance that my mom is taking care of my needs in this way." You would think, "Score! I'm going to wear my favorite shirt today!" And then you would go about your day.

But what about Mom's perspective? Mom is doing the extra laundry, week after week, and taking on the responsibility for her grown-up daughter's clean clothing needs. She's feeling resentful and frustrated that this grown woman has not taken responsibility for her own life, even though she's told her time and time again that she needs to. Why doesn't she see that Mom shouldn't be doing her laundry? If she loved her mom, she would step up! So, sadly, Mom continues to do her laundry and feels victimized by her daughter.

This situation is out of balance. So, whose responsibility is it to "fix" the imbalance? Well, if I'm the one who wakes up to a closet full of clean clothes, I'm not likely to ask you to stop doing my laundry. Why would I? My needs are being met, so I'm good to go.

Clearly, the person who is feeling out of balance needs to take responsibility for the imbalance. If doing someone else's laundry is disrupting your happiness, you must take responsibility for your own experience and require a change of yourself.

There are multiple benefits to taking responsibility for your own experience. Not only do you begin to create better-feeling days for yourself, you also provide powerful opportunities for those around you.

When I have the courage to take care of myself:

- ♦ I give permission to others to do the same. We stop the circle of obligation and begin to relate to each other authentically.

- ♦ I give you the opportunity to become a powerful problem solver and creator. I show you that I trust your ability to take care of yourself, even if you're not sure you can.

- ♦ I set an example for self-love, self-care, and taking personal responsibility; others can learn and grow from that example.

- ♦ I maintain my own energy balance, allowing me to live in joy and give from overflow, as opposed to obligation. Now I give because I want to and it feels good, not because it's expected or because I need the acknowledgment.

Reciprocal responsibility allows us to take care of our own needs and trust that others can do the same. We recognize that imbalance in relationships doesn't feel good and robs us of the time and energy to effectively take care of ourselves. By asserting this new understanding, we create a dynamic in which each person can feel powerful and capable, and we require each individual to take responsibility for himself or herself.

Potential, Passion, and Possibilities

We are infinitely powerful creators. We have the ability to be and experience anything we wish. You see that potential in your children, but do you see it in yourself? Are you embracing your potential?

Childhood is full of goal-setting, achievement, and dreams. Passion abounds. This dreaming and creating continues throughout school. Each stage of development provides the building block for the next set of goals. In middle school, we prepare for the goal of high school. In high school and college, we lay the foundation for our future. We take steps each day toward the goal of designing our adulthood.

It's no wonder that many people begin to struggle in their mid-twenties through mid-forties. There seems to be a finish line in there. You've achieved what you've set out to achieve and you reach a point of "now what?" The problem then becomes that you're so busy maintaining the results of your previous dreams, that you don't have the energy or insights to begin reaching for new ones.

For example, growing up, you may have had dreams of going to college, getting a job in your selected field, getting married, and having children. Now you've achieved all those goals, and you're amidst the chaos of balancing work, marriage, kids, activities, and self. You've created the life of your dreams, yet emotionally, you're drained, disengaged, unfulfilled, and confused.

Creating and achieving goals electrifies passion. The reason that so many of us fall into a rut of discontent is that we lose sight of setting new goals and activating our dreams. Yes, we're passionate about our kids and our work and our families, but we must continue to set and achieve personal goals rooted in passion. We are creators. We are designed to create new experiences and continually grow. When we stop creating, we feel the loss and sense the missing element in our lives.

Our souls recognize this need for passion and expansion. It's the reason that overloaded moms decide to go back to school or take on that extra project. We need the challenge and the excitement. When we can become aware of this need, we can orchestrate passion and new creation into our lives from a place of joy and possibilities while maintaining control of our experiences.

We can set an example of life-long achievement and continual goal setting. We show our children that passion and excitement for life continues past the traditionally scripted experience of school, career, partnership, and family. Never-ending possibilities and experiences are available to us. We want our children to experience everything they desire, so it is important for us to honor our own need to continuously evolve.

You may be reading this and thinking, "Yeah, that's all well and good, but I'm already in the rut. It's deep and scary and I don't even know what my passion is or when the heck I'd find time to explore it anyway." That's okay. There's no deadline. The process of falling in love with yourself, of learning about who you are and what you want, is just that… a process.

The first step here is to be thankful for the awareness. "Wow! I didn't realize that I'm not actively working on my goals or passions. How cool to now know that this is important to me." From there, you can begin to think about new goals and how you might integrate these new understandings in your life.

We'll talk more about goal-setting and getting out of the rut in Chapter Two.

2

The Self-Love Revolution

My hope is that you now understand why it is so important for you to take on the journey of self-love. This can feel like a tall order that requires intense effort and focus. This chapter introduces some strategies and perspectives to help you along the way. The journey to unconditional self-love is never-ending, and we accept the challenge knowing that all good journeys take a bit of effort. I assure you that it is worth the investment—you are worth the investment—and you deserve the joy and love that results from this undertaking.

As moms, we have a certain degree of pre-programming that leads us to be nurturing, teaching, and guiding. We use these qualities to take care of others, and often gauge our self worth on our ability to make the people around us comfortable and happy. Meanwhile, our own self often goes under-nurtured, forgotten, criticized, and abused.

Knowing that I am the primary role model for my kids, the need to fall completely and totally in love with myself seems clear. If I want to raise children who are confident, happy, passionate, and engaged, I need to show them what that looks like.

I realize that many of you will take steps toward self-love because you believe your kids deserve a strong, happy, joyful mom. My hope is that at some point in the adventure, you begin to believe and embrace the understanding that you deserve to be the strong, confident, happy person you are designed to be.

The Inner Child

On my own journey, the philosophy of the inner child has given me the insights and understandings to make giant changes in my relationship with myself. My operating system prior to this understanding was a militant disciplinarian. I required myself to behave in a certain way, and if I fell short of my own expectations or received any external criticism, I would beat myself up, feel terrible about who I am, wonder what was wrong with me, and reinforce the messages that I was just not good enough, not loveable, and pretty much useless.

It was easy for me to abuse the adult piece of me. Certainly, I had made enough mistakes throughout my life to deserve the criticism. The thought of loving the adult me seemed unreasonable. How could I love this mess of a woman? And beyond that, why would I love her?

Then I had a daughter. A beautiful, perfect, innocent, precious daughter.

I became aware of the possibility that she could someday feel about herself the way that I felt about myself. The thought of my precious daughter looking in the mirror and seeing anything but pure love and perfection broke my heart.

In that moment I realized that the beautiful, perfect, innocent, precious daughter is me. I am not only the daughter of my parents, but also a child of God. I couldn't see it in my adult reflection, but when I looked a little deeper, I could connect with the child within me. My adult self could handle the abuse that I threw at her. The child inside didn't deserve it.

Within each of us, the innocent remains. That small wide-eyed girl who soaked in all the details of her world.

The child who was simply experimenting with life and continuously learning based on how each experience played out. The child who looked for the approval of her parents and peers and wanted nothing more than to be loved, acknowledged and accepted.

That piece of you that wants nothing more than to be loved, acknowledged, and accepted remains. That little girl is still a part of you. The great news is that she no longer needs to rely on the love and acceptance of others. The little girl inside of you simply longs for your love and acceptance.

Take a minute to think about some of the messages that you send to yourself on a daily basis. These habitual thought patterns indicate what you believe about yourself. Would you say these things to your child? Would you want your child to say these things to him/herself?

What about when you're in a challenging situation? When you ask yourself for advice, is it the same advice you would give a friend? Or are you more demanding and harsh with yourself?

I invite you to take some time to meet the little girl inside of you. Think about who you are at the center of your being. Look into your eyes and allow yourself to see the pureness that remains. The small child with the curious spirit and the shining smile. The innocent who is free from guilt and expectation with the limitless imagination and ability to see all possibilities. The boundless source of love, energy, and joy that has always been with you, whether you've realized it or not. She is still available to you and ready to play.

Falling in love with my inner child and embracing her perfection was the single most influential shift I've made in my life. The ability to be gentle with myself in all circumstances and love myself unconditionally has opened possibilities and joy that I had never imagined. I was able to discover and nurture my adult side only after I discovered and began to nurture my inner child.

Embracing All the Pieces

As human beings, we are complex and multifaceted. We feel emotions and create experiences without limit. We are also highly programmable. The process of childhood has a distinct purpose: to help a child learn the traditions and beliefs of the society. Because the adults are the critical role models that the child observes and emulates, the child develops an understanding of good versus bad, acceptable versus unacceptable, lovable versus unlovable.

Along this journey, we begin to judge our experiences and emotions based on the interpretations of those around us and the consequences of each situation. We look to expand our "good" traits to become "better" and we look to minimize our "bad" qualities. We label each piece of ourselves with systematic precision to help orchestrate our experiences. When I use my "good" qualities, I am a good person, loved and accepted. When I use my "bad" qualities, I am judged and rejected.

As we become more self aware and philosophically savvy, the practice of expanding the good and denouncing the bad becomes problematic. Here's why. We are all of it. We are the good, the neutral, and the "bad" qualities. Within each of us is the sinner and the saint, the bully and the victim, the neat freak and the slob, the conformist and the rebel, the alpha and the omega, and everything in between. All of these pieces are within each of us.

We may operate more often from a particular set of traits. We may deny certain characteristics while celebrating others. But because all of them are within us, given the right situation, we can act from every one of these qualities.

The range of characteristics available to us is easy to observe in children. We can see the growth of certain traits and the experimentation with others. This process of experimentation leads us to strengthen our connection with certain parts of ourselves and disconnect from less desirable parts. Even though adults may not associate with the disconnected parts, or may think we can cast them aside, their presence remains.

The journey to unconditional self-love requires us to love all of our parts. Not just the ones we consider good or positive, but truly all the pieces within us. Remember the child inside of us who just wants to be loved and acknowledged? You can think of the countless pieces of you in the same way. Each just wants to be loved and accepted for who it is. Each wants to operate in perfect harmony with its neighbors and with you.

We refer to this "shadow side" as those traits and emotions that we have judged to be bad. It's the "dark side" of our personality. It's that piece that sneaks out periodically (usually at the most inopportune times) and embarrasses us with its socially unacceptable outburst. It's the piece that takes over when we are feeling out of control and don't understand where a particular behavior is coming from.

Embracing your shadow is an exercise in awareness, acceptance, and expansion. Several steps can help you love your shadow.

1. First, start recognizing the pieces of you that you are denying. A good way to begin is by observing what traits irritate you in your friends, family, and co-workers. If you can get onboard with the fact that we are all of it, then the icky thing that you are noticing in someone else is also within you.

2. Next, claim that trait as being part of you.

3. Declare your love for that piece and thank it for the contribution it has made in helping you become who you are.

4. Celebrate your new awareness and the feel the gratitude to yourself for taking another step in the effort to love yourself completely.

Let's walk through the process with a couple examples.

Example One: The cashier at the grocery store is rude to you.

1. Begin by noticing that she's behaved rudely, and that is just one small piece of who she is.

2. Next, make a declaration about yourself. "I know that there is a piece of me that is rude." Own it! It's true. The harder it is to own the particular trait, the greater the denial of that part of yourself, and an indication of how much that piece is being unloved.

3. From there, accept and love that piece. "I love the part of me that is rude. It is part of who I am and it's okay to be me." Be thankful for your awareness of rudeness and the gifts that that awareness brings. Because you've been working to not behave from a place of rudeness, you have developed behaviors and mannerisms that are normally kind and gentle.

4. Celebrate! Wow, it's such a gift to be who I am and to have the awareness I have.

Example Two: You snap at your child when he/she asks you a question.

1. Try not to justify the behavior, simply recognize that there is a piece of you that is harsh. Remember, it is not all of who you are, it is just a piece of you.

2. Own that piece of yourself. "There is a piece of me that is harsh. I am harsh."

3. "I love and accept the piece of me that is harsh. It's part of who I am and it's okay to be me."

4. Celebrate! Wow, it's such a gift to be who I am and to have the awareness I have.

When we actively begin to love and accept all of the pieces of ourselves, these pieces are less likely to disrupt our joy and experiences. It is the denial of these traits that causes them to come out in ways that seem out of control. When we honor and accept the emotions and characteristics within us, our self judgment lessens and we can operate from a place of authenticity and love.

As parents, we can also help our children to understand the varying aspects of themselves. Here are some things to practice.

- ◆ Look for discipline strategies that do not utilize shame and guilt.
- ◆ Remind your kids that you love them completely, not just the "good" parts.
- ◆ Allow your children to experience the feelings of the different parts of themselves, and solicit their thoughts about them.
- ◆ Use questions so that your kids can think for themselves and determine what feels better for them.
    - ◆ How did that feel for you?
    - ◆ What do you think you could have done instead?
    - ◆ What would feel good to do next?
- ◆ Model your own process of acceptance when you become aware of a denied part of yourself.

If you are interested in learning more about shadow work, *The Dark Side of the Light Chasers* by Debbie Ford is an excellent resource.

Commit to Self-love!

Now that we have explored the idea of self-love and its importance not only for you, but also for your children, it is time to take action.

I encourage you to make a vow to yourself right here and right now. I invite you to begin taking the steps to build a positive and loving relationship with yourself that is free from abuse, sabotage, guilt, and regret.

This is not a one-time offering. This vow is designed to be renewed on a regular basis and strengthened with perseverance, trust, and gentleness. The little girl inside of you deserves your love, attention, and appreciation. The adult you can provide it. Please don't wait.

> I hereby vow to love and honor myself as a Divine being, a child of God. I vow to never again use my thoughts and actions as a weapon against myself regardless of the events or decisions involved. I will be gentle with myself if I fall into old habits.
>
> I will apologize for the self abuse, recommit to a life of unconditional love, and continue to move forward.

I vow to take care of the little girl inside
of me with the same enthusiasm and
love with which I care for others. I trust
that each person I come in contact with
has this same ability to take perfect care
of themselves.

I vow to honor the decisions I make,
knowing that I made them with good
intentions. Each decision either brings
the desired outcome or an experience
from which to learn and grow.

I vow to recommit to myself each time I
become aware that I am not operating
from a place of pure self-love and joy. I
will celebrate the steps that I am taking
and continue building my belief that I
am magnificent, beautiful and enough
just as I am right now.

Taking this vow, you embark on the journey to complete
self-love and acceptance. Along the way, you enjoy
continuous opportunities for celebrating progress,

realigning with the importance of the process, and deepening your understandings.

I invite you to hold a commitment ceremony for yourself. Give yourself a ring, crystal, necklace, bracelet, or other symbol to remind yourself of your vow and to represent the love that you are pledging to yourself. If you are willing, have the ceremony with your family or friends to share the gift of your vow. Offer them suggestions for how they can support you on your journey. Share with them why this commitment is so important to you and what you hope the result will be.

Becoming your own partner is the ultimate gift. It is a powerful exercise that allows you to see from a new perspective, honor your unique talents and passions, and live with love, joy, and gratitude. Anyone can make this commitment and experience the shift to self-love.

As you continue to reaffirm your self-love, include your kids in the process. Share with them how exciting it is to be you, and remind them how lucky they are to be who they are. If you hear your child criticizing herself, help her see the learning in the situation and how great it is to be able to learn and grow each day. Practice maintaining a positive perspective in your home, so that you continue the momentum of love and joy.

Rediscovering Passion and Goal-Setting

Because setting and achieving new goals is an integral part of a passionate, engaging life, it makes sense to look at a simple process for getting where you want to go.

The first step in goal setting is determining the goal. It is quite common for us to go through life on a day-to-day basis without any destination in mind. We make moment-to-moment decisions without guidelines or determining factors, and then one day we look up and find ourselves lost. How did I arrive at this place in life?

It's no different than a road trip. If you set out on a journey with no destination in mind, and you turn here and there with no particular rhyme or reason, you can't know where you will end up. Right? Life works the same way. If you have no plan for where you're going, you have little control over where you will end up or what you might experience along the way.

But, if you set out on a road trip with a clear destination, you will make decisions along the way that lead you there. You may experience a detour, or a wrong turn, or an unexpected storm, but your destination is set and your determination to arrive is unwavering. You will get there; nothing can stop you.

I invite you to think about goal setting in the same way. If I have a goal, and my intention is to achieve that goal, the decisions I make on a day-to-day basis will either align with that goal, thus bringing me one step closer to achievement, or they will be out of alignment with my goal, leading me on a detour or off the trail completely.

One very cool aspect of living from a goal perspective is that you always have a basis from which to make decisions. When faced with a decision, we can ask, "Does this choice align with my goal?" If the answer is yes, then we know it is the right decision for us. If the answer is no, then we have a really good reason to not make that particular choice. When we become aware of these thought processes, any choice that is out of alignment with our goal is a choice to sabotage our desires and a concrete breach of self-love.

We deserve to achieve our goals. It is our birthright to create the life of our dreams. We are the only obstacle to that achievement.

Once you've created a rut in your life, it can be difficult to even entertain the possibility of achieving your dreams—you simply do not know what they are anymore. You have forgotten what you're passionate about.

I invite you to play with the goal-setting process with the intention of falling completely and totally in love with yourself. It is the greatest gift you can offer to yourself and your children, and will start you back on the journey of living a passionate and joyful life filled with dreams come true.

So, here's how the process works:

- ◆ **Set the goal**: Fall completely and unconditionally in love with yourself.

- ◆ **Become aware**: Begin looking for behaviors and decisions that are out of alignment with this goal.

- ◆ **Celebrate your awareness**: Use these observations as an opportunity to celebrate new learning.

- ◆ **Hold the focus**: Achieving a goal requires ongoing focus. If your goal was to get a college degree, you would need to continually recommit to that goal until you've achieved it. The same commitment is required here. Remind yourself as often as necessary about your goal and the importance of achieving it.

- ◆ **Take action**: Take one easy, joyful step in the direction of your dream. Have fun with the journey. Upon completion of your first step, determine what your next step will be. You do not need to know anything more than your very next step. I guarantee that when you complete the step you are on, you will know what step to take next.

- **Celebrate your action**: Acknowledge yourself for moving toward your dream. Nothing can stop you. You are powerful and you're doing it!

- **Realign as necessary with gentleness and love**: If you become aware that you've lost focus on your goal, use it as an opportunity to stop, reaffirm your goal, and then determine your next step.

- **Look for learning**: Throughout this process, become aware of what you're learning about yourself and your operating system. The point of life is to learn, so don't forget to watch for the lessons that present themselves along the way.

When you recognize the need to follow your passion and achieve goals, you begin living from a place of creating and expansion. You show your children that learning and following your heart never stops. You play an active role in the unfolding of your life and enjoy feelings of achievement and success. Isn't that what you want for your kids? A life of dreams come true via focus, inspired action, and learning.

3

New Thinking for a New Generation

Now that you have an understanding of the importance of self-love, how it affects your kids, and some strategies for improving your relationship with yourself, we're ready to move on to another thought shift. From the perspective of self-love, some of your "go-to" thoughts and behaviors will also begin to change. This chapter suggests some new ideas to consider.

The New Role of Guilt

One common concern for moms as they're learning about self-love is that if I put my own needs first and take care of myself, I'll feel guilty for it. For many, guilt is a daily emotion that drives the bulk of their decision making.

Here's a big statement: Guilt is the most overused and misunderstood emotion in our society. How many times a day do you feel guilty about something? We feel guilty if we eat the wrong food. Guilty if we say the wrong thing. Guilty if we make a decision. Guilty if we don't make a decision. Guilty if someone we're associated with feels guilty.

Sidebar story: One time, my friend's husband accidentally stepped on my sunglasses and broke them. My friend felt very guilty. Huh? She wasn't even in the room at the time.

It appears to me that momhood amps up the guilt for many of us. It's almost as if this ridiculous emotion somehow bonds us in a common experience of feeling badly.

We've been conditioned to take care of everybody else's feelings and make decisions that won't hurt anyone around us. So, any time that someone else's feelings are shaken, we take responsibility for it and feel guilty. We become so fearful of the guilt we might feel that we lose the ability to make decisions and take care of ourselves. What we are actually guilty of is not taking responsibility for the one and only thing we can actually control—our own feelings.

To examine whether you are overplaying your guilt card, let's try a little game of "Guilty or Not Guilty," shall we?

> **Situation**: You accidentally break something that belongs to someone else.
>
> **Action**: You apologize and offer to replace / fix the item.
>
> **Verdict**: Not guilty! You didn't intend to hurt someone, and you made an effort to make it right.
>
> **Situation**: You are invited to two events on the same day.
>
> **Action**: You attend one of the events and respect-fully decline the other.
>
> **Verdict**: Not guilty! You get to decide where you spend your time. Seriously, you can't be in two places at once.

Situation: You are angry with someone.

Action: You intentionally harm them or their possessions because they must pay for making you angry.

Verdict: Guilty. You intended for something bad to happen and took action.

Situation: Your partner/friend/co-worker does something that has a negative effect on something or someone else.

Verdict: Not guilty! The situation has nothing to do with you.

Situation: You forget to send snack on your kid's snack day.

Action: Upon realizing you forgot, you send a snack the next day with a note of apology.

Verdict: Not guilty! In the grand scheme of things, how important is this? You made up for the oversight. It's okay to move on without feeling badly.

Situation: You make a decision that is right for you.

Action: You do what is best for you and trust that anyone else involved will either understand or get over it.

Verdict: Not guilty! It is your number one responsibility to take care of you. If we all took care of our own feelings, there would be a whole lot fewer hurt feelings in the world.

These scenarios are very simple and clear. So is every scenario in your life if you step back and look at it from this fresh perspective. Unless your intention was to deliberately harm someone, your guilt is misplaced. Rather than choosing guilt, you can actively shift your default emotion to:

- ◆ *Observation* – Notice what role you are playing and where you can own your experience.

- ◆ *Learning* – What can you learn from the situation?

- ◆ *Expansion* – Can you gain new insights and understand more?

- ♦ ***Wonderment*** – Wow! I wonder why that happened.
- ♦ ***Self-love*** – Every situation is an opportunity to fall more in love with you.

Where do you land on the guilt scale? Is it time to find a new default emotion? Bottom line here is that it is okay for you to be you. If you are generally operating from a place of love, you have nothing to feel guilty about, and the energy you are wasting on that guilt would be better spent on something that feels good. Remember the idea of watering the weeds? If guilt is ruling your emotional garden, it may be time to do something about it.

And what about being that critical role model for your kids? Should your kids feel guilty for taking care of themselves or making decisions in their own best interests? Did you learn your hypersensitive guilt skills from your mom? Oops! She just didn't know that there was another option. You do! And the investment you make in yourself will benefit everyone around you.

Rethinking Guilt

If it is important for you to allow guilt to play an active role in your decision-making process, I invite you to turn the tables. Rather than feeling guilty for not meeting the needs of others or not protecting their feelings or not reading their minds, what if you felt guilty only when you failed to meet your own needs?

Your new understanding of your inner child and the importance of honoring yourself comes with a responsibility to take care of yourself and make decisions that uphold your self-love vow. Allow this awareness to be your driving force for decision-making.

A client recently shared with me that she was out with some friends, and one of the friends asked her to have a martini with her. My client, Jamie, really doesn't like martinis and wanted something else. But Jamie was afraid she would feel guilty if she denied the friend, so she got the martini.

In this situation, what if Jamie had had the tools to put her own needs first instead of attempting to proactively protect her friend's feelings? What if, instead of fearing that she would hurt the friend, Jamie realized that she would hurt her own feelings if she didn't honor her desires? And what if Jamie's kids saw their mom take perfect care of herself?

It is possible to eliminate feelings of guilt from your day-to-day experience. However, if you need a stepping-stone process to start with, I invite you to utilize your highly crafted guilt skills to advance the mission of taking perfect care of yourself. Use them to create new behavior and thought patterns that acknowledge and protect you.

Celebrating Success and Celebrating Learning

One key mindset that can help you put your guilt-ridden experience behind you is to explore the idea that there are no mistakes. Everything we do creates an opportunity for learning, and one of our main objectives—if not the only objective—here on earth is to learn. Every experience creates one of two outcomes: an opportunity to celebrate or an opportunity to learn (which, in my opinion, is also cause for celebration).

When we begin to see our decisions from the viewpoint of celebration and learning, we remove the need for guilt and regret. There is no cause for regret because we got exactly what we were supposed to get from the situation. It either played out in the way we had intended, or it provided the opportunity to think some more about it. Why did it work out the way it did? What can we learn from the situation? This extra thinking provides new information and insights that we can use to create our next experience.

Looking back on your childhood, what would have been different if your parents had encouraged you to view your decisions from a place of celebrating success and celebrating learning?

When we begin to see our children in their perfection, we allow their natural gifts and innate knowledge to lead the way. We help them to stay in alignment with their natural self-love, so they make decisions in their best interests. All of their experiences can be seen as celebrations and opportunities for growth. How do we do this? We reclaim the natural self-love, innocence, and curiosity we had as children.

The reality is that the only person I truly control is me. I can interact with my children in ways that I feel will make a difference to them, but at the end of the day, the only behavior I truly control is my own. The more I focus on developing my insights and understandings, the more I allow my kids to joyfully learn and expand. I take on the responsibility for parenting myself and continuing my journey as a learner. I look at all situations as an opportunity to experiment and grow.

Because I do this for myself, I teach my children how easy, fun and exciting life is. I show them I can handle anything that comes my way and that I can learn from it and then create whatever I want to experience next.

Amazingly Special Kids

We've come a long way in our understanding of parenting. We've learned from trial and error, and witnessed polarized philosophies about how best to raise children. The reality is new variables come into play with each generation. This Google/Facebook generation has challenges and rewards that are not covered in the "when I was a kid" parenting style.

The art of being a mom has also evolved considerably. Not too long ago, women had pretty limited life path options. You could become a mom, a teacher, a secretary, or a nurse. Today, for us and our children, the options are limitless. The experience of life can be whatever we decide to make it. We, as moms, can take certain steps to help our kids achieve their dreams and live a life of joy and enthusiasm.

The first step is to realize a few things about your kids. Children…

- ♦ are born with everything they need to be happy and successful.
- ♦ have an innate spiritual connection and at their core are pure love and joy.
- ♦ are so much smarter and in tune with truth and reality than we can even imagine.
- ♦ have an ability and desire to feel good about themselves, share their unique talents, and create a life that is filled with passion and abundance.
- ♦ learn how life works from the experiences they have, as well as those they witness.
- ♦ have the need to feel powerful, capable, and connected.

Next, realize that all of these things are true about you, too. You have everything you need inside of you, and you have an innate ability to know truth and joy and love. You have unique gifts and a need to feel powerful, capable, and connected.

The philosophy is simple. Kids learn from their experiences and the example they witness. We all want our kids to feel good about themselves and see their value and awesomeness. Therefore, we as moms must see our own value and awesomeness and feel good about ourselves *and each other*. This small detail may be what creates the tipping point in our understanding.

The process of falling in love with yourself is not a competition with other moms. In fact, as we feel better and better about who we are and the role we play in our kids' lives, we empower other moms to learn and build their confidence as well.

Imagine for a minute how brightly our world will shine when each of us...

- celebrates who we are.
- honors the gifts of those around us.
- shows our kids that everyone deserves to experience passion, love, joy, and success.
- believes that we alone are the sole decision maker in whether or not that is our experience.

We, as moms, have the opportunity to create this reality. We can celebrate life. We can understand our experiences in a new way—a way filled with learning, love, and excitement. We can begin to see ourselves from a perspective of kindness and nurturing. And we can set an example for our kids that allows them to soar beyond what we can even imagine. Tall order? Nope. Just do your part for you, the rest will unfold on its own.

The New Role of Parenting

So with our new understanding of personal responsibility and parenting from the perspective of self-love comes a role reversal of sorts. I encourage you to become a student of your child and actively look for what you can learn about emotions, behavior, and the joy of life. Take a stance of curiosity and observation. What can you learn from your kids?

As you take on the role of student, you create an amazing dynamic with your children to share what you're noticing. By acknowledging their ability to take care of themselves and understand their own power, we parent from a place of joy and engagement.

When you accept the responsibility to fall in love with yourself, you set an example of how to take care of yourself and how to maintain your personal power in all situations. We are truly never without choices, and showing our children the tools they can use to make decisions is a tremendous gift. The catch is that we first have to develop the tools and practice ourselves.

As much as you can, I invite you to get out of the way of your kids. They are so perfectly equipped to live amazing lives. They can achieve anything that they desire; and so can you. All the energy that you are investing in helping your kids learn about life may be clouding what they already know internally.

With all the extra energy you save from not having to program your kids, you gain all the resources you need to re-program yourself to a place of deserving, self-love, and joy. The little girl inside of you needs it so much more than your kids do. A happier you will parent from a happier place, allowing your kids to maintain the innocence and participatory learning that comes with childhood.

4

I t is likely that changing your operating system from one of taking care of others to taking care of yourself will cause some shake-up. When one's laundry fairy goes away, one might resort to all kinds of interesting tactics to try to get her back. Being equipped to make changes with confidence, as well handle whatever reactions you receive, can help you stay focused and maintain your position of self-love.

We are all equipped with emotional "toolboxes." We use the tools we have to address and move through whatever situation we're in. You can consciously add tools to your toolbox by anticipating the reactions you might receive. Because you now realize how important these behavior shifts are for you and your kids, it is equally important to feel powerful enough to implement them. In this section, we'll look at how to start operating from self-love, some of the reactions to watch out for, and the tools you need to move through the process.

Super-Easy Places to Start

If you are the mom who takes care of everything and everybody, here are some quick, easy ways for you to begin to adjust your behavior from one of constant service to others, to one of self-love.

Reclaim Some Personal Space and Balance

♦ Lock the bathroom door. It is okay for you to have some time to yourself.

♦ Eat your dinner while it is hot. A great response to put in your toolbox is, "I would be happy to get that for you just as soon as I'm done with my food." This response works well for many situations. You don't have to be interrupted. What you are working on (whatever it is) is important, too.

♦ Balance is not an option; it's a requirement. You get to decide how much of your time and energy are allocated to the various aspects of your life. Stop putting yourself last; it doesn't help anybody in the long run.

- ◆ Ask yourself, "What do I want?"
- ◆ Remember that you always have choices. Can you choose something that feels better?

Play!

- ◆ Your kids are only going to be kids for a very short time. Enjoy them. Remember, you can learn so much from observing their brilliance.
- ◆ Just because you're a parent doesn't mean that you can't have fun. Make time to enjoy your partner, your friends, and yourself. Create a list of things you enjoy doing and make it a priority to do them.
- ◆ Anything you do can be enjoyable if you decide that it is. Incorporate play, laughter, and fun into your daily routine. Sing in the shower. Dance while you do the dishes. Laugh at the dinner table. What we focus on expands. If you focus on enjoying yourself, you will continue to enjoy yourself. Hooray!

Boundaries

One of the greatest self-care tools is the ability to set appropriate boundaries. We often think that setting boundaries is about saying "no," but it is really much more than that. It's about how we prioritize the needs that surround us every day. It's about saying "yes" to ourselves and honoring the limited amount of time and energy that we have. More than that, it's about showing our kids that taking care of our own needs is not negotiable.

We've looked at the importance of trusting that others are capable and perfectly equipped to meet their own needs. It's worth repeating. Just as you are perfectly able to take care of you, the people around you are equally capable. The difference is that they might not know it yet! If you've been actively meeting needs for them, they may have become dependent on you. They may even push the envelope and continuously ask you to meet more of their needs.

Now that you understand how critical it is for you to take care of yourself, it's time to begin doing it. The laws of physics dictate the number of hours in a day and how much we can do in those hours. Become aware of where you invest your energy each day. Which areas feel good? Which are obligations or expectations? Where would you like to invest more? What are you ready to let go?

- ◆ Say "No." Supermom is an illusion, and you are way too valuable to waste energy on things that don't matter. It's okay to start slowly and pick one easy thing to take off your plate. Take the time to celebrate how amazing it feels, and then do it again!

- ◆ Get real! Take a look at the balance of responsibility in your home. Is it out of whack? If you're doing more than your fair share, it is your responsibility to make changes to your contribution.

- ◆ Let go of judgment. Allow yourself to do things that you want to do, not only the things you should or "have" to do. In reality, you don't "have" to do anything… what you do is always a choice!

You are responsible for you. This includes your thoughts, your feelings, and your actions. Setting boundaries is a commitment to protecting yourself. It's about letting in what feels good, and stopping things that don't. As you become more aware of where you allocate your time and energy, you can begin to make adjustments.

A great place to start is with your daily schedule. What are you doing that doesn't have value to you? What can you delegate to others? Is there a balance of giving and receiving? If there is no receiving, and lots of giving, that's a problem.

It's okay to start small. As you get stronger, it will get easier to ask others to contribute. It will get easier to say "no" to things that don't feel good. You always have a choice. You can choose to take on more and more, or you can choose to honor yourself.

The practice of boundaries is a great parenting tool, as well. I try to give my kids the space they need to feel powerful, make choices, and learn about life. This is not, however, an invitation to a free-for-all. As I am parenting, I ask myself how the situation feels for me. Here are some of the ways that boundaries help me create a good home atmosphere.

I set boundaries for:

- **Appropriate behavior in our home**. It doesn't feel good to me if my kids are jumping on furniture, screaming, or glued to the TV. I say things like, "That's not working for me; please choose something else." Or, "You are welcome to go in the playroom or outside to jump around."

- **The communication style that I respond to**. I am sensitive to how others talk to me. I don't do well with whining, sassiness, or demanding. "Is there a question you'd like to ask me?" and "I would be happy to talk to you when your voice sounds like mine" are responses that I use to help my kids honor my boundaries. This allows me to remain in control of how I'm feeling.

- **Making a contribution to the family**. Helping children feel like a part of the family unit is important. We each have a role to play. Even small kids can take on roles such as trash helper, laundry assistant, mail getter, plant waterer, silverware sorter, etc. Are you hogging all the roles? Determining tasks that belong specifically to each of your kids can help foster a team environment. You can then set boundaries by allowing your family members to do their part. I love the statement, "I love you all the time, but we have a lot more fun when you're on my team!"

- **Safety and health**. I use boundaries to help teach my kids basic safety and healthy living. Rather than operating from a controlling objective, I use it as a love reminder. "I love you so much, and I want your body to be healthy. What did you do to stay healthy and safe today?"

Setting boundaries at home is only part of the job. If you habitually take on more and more, it is probably time to set some boundaries in your obligations, as well. It really is okay to say "no." Do not feel guilty for taking care of yourself.

Reactions from Others

On the journey to self-love, moms report some common experiences. Let's look at what you might expect to hear when your friends and family learn that you are no longer sacrificing your own needs to take responsibility for theirs.

Guilt: Here it is again. When we are new to taking care of ourselves, it is easy to fall into the guilt trap. Loved ones who know you well will feed that guilt monster to try to maintain the status quo and royal treatment they are accustomed to receiving from you. This is in an attempt to avoid meeting their own needs; it is not about you! (See Chapter Three for a guilt reminder.)

Manipulation: Usually goes hand in hand with guilt, but be on the lookout for excuses, bribery, and attempts to convince you that you are necessary to the other person's survival.

Anger: Upon losing the valuable gift of your dispro-portionate time and energy, others may direct anger toward you. This anger is a good sign that you are officially putting your needs first, and also an indication of how necessary your new actions are. If it makes others angry that you are no longer willing to sacrifice your own well-being for theirs, clearly the lesson in self-care applies to all parties involved.

Withdrawal: If in your relationships, you typically give while others take, you may begin to experience less of a connection with them. As you build your self-love and personal care strategies, you will be able to see clearly if your relationships are in balance. Are there people in your life who are connected to you only because you give yourself away? From your new position of self-love, you can now require an equal and joy-based relationship.

Tools for Maintaining Self-love Under Pressure

Now that you're aware of some of the reactions you might face, let's look at how you can maintain your commitment to yourself and trust that you're doing the right thing. Having a well-stocked toolbox is the best way to ensure the process of falling in love with yourself stays on track.

"Go to" phrases — Having several rehearsed, positive responses in your back pocket is one powerful strategy. Make them your own, and use them instead of engaging in negative or combative conversations. Here are a few to get you thinking:

- ◆ "I can't wait to see how you solve that problem for yourself."
- ◆ "Wow! It sounds like you're really feeling _____. What do you think you're going to do?"
- ◆ "Isn't it fun that we're learning to do things in a different way?"

Timeout — When faced with a situation that is charged with emotion, give yourself permission to take a timeout instead of engaging in combat. Remove yourself from the conversation, and request that it continue when both parties are better equipped to communicate from a place of love and authenticity.

Pay Attention to Progression — There is a cumulative effect that happens with emotional behaviors and new awareness. A build-up of unresolved small issues can lead to an explosion. Allow yourself to become aware of the small issues and address them as they occur. Recommit to yourself, and remind yourself how important you are and how much you deserve to meet your own needs.

Self-love is Not Selfish — One great guilt / manipulation tactic is the ever popular, "I can't believe you're being so selfish!" It is important to reiterate how self-love and self-care are actually the opposite of selfishness.

Remember the selfishness points discussed in Chapter One.

- ◆ Operating from selfishness takes from others to meet ones needs; self-love requires me to take responsibility for my own needs.

- ◆ Selfishness holds others responsible for my feelings; self-love realizes I control my feelings and reactions.

- ◆ Selfishness believes that others are required to take care of me and make me happy; self-love allows me to be happy regardless of external circumstances.

♦ Self-love trusts that those around me are capable of taking perfect care of themselves.

Should you be accused of selfishness, please remember that self-love is the greatest gift you can give to both yourself and those around you. You might consider a response such as, "I understand that it feels different for you now that I'm not taking on responsibility for your happiness. I'm so excited for you to discover how to take care of yourself and find joy within you! I want so much for you to be happy and powerful, and you are the only one who can make that happen for you. And I am the only one who can make it happen for me. Isn't that cool?"

Learning Out Loud

As you are walking the journey to self-love, I encourage you to make observations about your progress to your kids. Open and honest conversations about what you are learning provide an opportunity for you and your kids to think about situations, feelings, and self-exploration in a new way.

It might sound something like this:

> **Mom**: "Hey, Nathan! Would you like to hear about something new that I'm learning?"
>
> **Nathan**: "Sure."
>
> **Mom**: "Well, I am learning to treat myself with love and respect. I didn't realize that sometimes I am really mean to myself. Isn't it neat that even when you grow up you still learn new stuff?"
>
> **Nathan**: "Yep."
>
> **Mom**: "What are you learning about you?"

When you have the courage to share your journey with your kids, they benefit from your learning. As a bonus, you get the opportunity to learn from them. Really listen to what they share with you. The insights and brilliance that comes from this kind of conversation will amaze you. You will gain information about how your kids are feeling, and create communication behaviors that provide the building blocks for future discussions.

Furthermore, working through your new thought processes out loud solidifies them within you. When you share with your kids that you are learning, you give them permission to learn. When you give them the opportunity to share what they are feeling, you create a safe place for talking about learning. We are not doing this in a behavioral correction sort of way. We are doing it in an exploratory, learn-about-yourself way.

Powerful Questions and Acknowledgment

Two great tools you can use in almost any situation are *asking questions* and *offering acknowledgment*. Asking questions gives other people the opportunity to think for themselves and feel heard. It takes us off the defensive and allows us to exchange ideas in a non-combative way. Using powerful questions works not only with your kids, but also with everyone you communicate with.

We talked earlier about the need to feel powerful. When we ask questions, we allow others to maintain their personal power. We demonstrate that we value their ideas.

Moreover, we create an atmosphere of acceptance and listening. We all want to feel heard. In addition, when we ask questions and honor others, they are much more likely to hear what we have to say as well.

Using questions takes the pressure off being "right" and allows for an exchange of ideas. The reason this so important for parents is that we know that kids will disagree for the sake of disagreement with much of what we say! Using questions is a smart way to let kids think for themselves without creating a debate situation.

Examples of powerful questions include:

- ♦ What do you think?
- ♦ How are you feeling about that?
- ♦ What are you planning to do next?
- ♦ How do you think that will work out?
- ♦ Are you open to some other ideas?
- ♦ Why do you think that happened?
- ♦ Did you learn anything new?

In addition to getting good at asking powerful questions, I invite you to become proficient in acknowledgment, as well. Acknowledgment is simply the act of highlighting the positive that you see in others or a situation. It is an indication that you are listening and creates an increase in positive momentum.

Here are some examples:

- I really like your idea about _____.
- I think it's neat that you are thinking about that!
- I want to acknowledge you for realizing that.
- It's so cool that you _____.
- Wow! That's interesting!
- Tell me more about _____.

Again, when we ask powerful questions and listen to the answers, we create a communication style that allows us to remain in control of our emotions, maintain our own energy, and operate from a place of self-love. All the while, we are also modeling for others how well it works.

You don't need to be a "think on your feet" kind of person to use these tools. You can memorize two or three of your favorites and use them over and over again. It's a simple way to take care of yourself while creating a safe place for others to do the same. The ultimate win-win.

The next time you feel yourself getting frustrated in a conversation, ask a powerful question. Listen for a way to acknowledge the other person. You'll be amazed how quickly the feeling of frustration returns to calm. Then congratulate yourself! What a beautiful sign of progress that you were able to take care of yourself and love yourself through a potentially troubling situation.

I CAn
do it.

5

Falling in Love with You — Suggested Exercises

This chapter gives several simple, fun exercises that you can do to build your self-love and turn negative self-talk into love-filled, self-honoring dialog. I recommend you read through all the exercises, and then determine which one feels like the most fun for you. Start there!

With anything we do, practice makes perfect. You can do the exercises in any order and repeat them as desired. The main objective is to become aware of how you are treating yourself, and then consciously decide to love yourself … all of the parts of you.

This is not, I repeat, *not* an opening for you to identify your shortcomings. Please be gentle with yourself as you walk through this process. Use it as an opportunity to build yourself up instead of kicking yourself around with degrading rants. ("Geez, I can't believe you're so stupid. You can't even do this simple exercise to make your life better. No wonder you're in the situations you're in. I don't know why you thought you're anything more than a _____"). Yep, I used to run those tapes, too.

Part of your commitment to falling in love with you involves changing those tapes. Before now, you simply didn't have the awareness, insights, or tools to create something different. There's no guilt here, no reason to punish yourself. Instead, use the opportunity to renew your commitment and rehearse new thought patterns.

Try these replacement thoughts:

- "Wow! I wonder why this exercise feels so difficult. I am so thankful to be building new awareness. I am so excited to continue practicing loving me."

- "I love that part of me that resists changing. I am so grateful that even after all these years of abusing myself, I now have this awareness and can create something new."

- "I'm so sorry for the way I've treated myself. I just didn't know how much I was hurting myself. What a blessing to be learning a new way of relating to me."

Become aware of the messages you are sending to your kids, as well. Those messages will likely become their thought patterns in the future. Are you sending messages of love and acceptance? As you work on changing your own thought tapes, you will be better equipped to help your kids develop positive and self-respecting thoughts. Again, this is not an invitation to beat up on yourself; it is an opportunity to move forward in a new and more joyful way with fresh insights and powerful tools.

Core Values

Starting on page 90, you will find a list of 160 core value words. You can also find this list at www.ilovememom.com.

Step One: Without over-thinking it, go through the list and circle or highlight any words that really resonate with you. Choose the words that "belong" to you. These words align with who you are at the core of your being. They represent what is important to you.

Step Two: Look at your circled words and narrow down that list to about 30 value words. Write those top 30 words on page 93.

Step Three: From that list of 30 value words, choose the 10 that feel like your most important or most closely aligned values. Write your top 10, ranked in order of importance to you, on page 94.

If you feel you are eliminating words that are important to you, don't worry. The reality is that each of us is ALL of these things (and millions more). Getting clear on your top 10 does not mean the other aspects of you are not important.

Step Four: Rank your list in order from 1 to 10, with 1 being your most important core value. Write those words on the lines at the bottom of page 95.

Step Five: Recite your values out loud. State: "I am _____, _____, _____," and so on. Bonus points if you are brave enough to share your list with another person. Saying these words aloud might feel weird. The purpose of this step is to really own your values, and to believe that they represent who you are at your core—the true you.

What you have just produced is an operating guide. You can use this list of core values in your decision-making process throughout the day. When faced with a difficult decision, recite your list. "I am _____, _____, _____, and so on, and because I am these things, the choice I make is _____." You can make the decision based on what is most important to you. Using this tool allows you to let go of outside influence, clear mental clutter, and rely on some simple guidelines for decision making.

I take Good
Care of Me.

My Core Values

Abundance
Acceptance
Accomplishment
Achievement
Acknowledgement
Adventure
Ambition
Appreciation
Approachability
Assertiveness
Attractiveness
Authenticity
Awareness
Balance
Beauty
Belonging
Bravery
Calmness
Charm
Cheerfulness
Clarity
Clear-mindedness
Comfort
Commitment
Compassion
Confidence
Connection
Consciousness

Courage
Creativity
Credibility
Curiosity
Dependability
Depth
Desire
Determination
Devotion
Dignity
Dreaming
Drive
Effectiveness
Efficiency
Elation
Empathy
Encouragement
Energy
Enjoyment
Enthusiasm
Excellence
Expertise
Expressiveness
Extroversion
Faith
Family
Fearlessness
Financial independence

My Core Values

Fitness	Inspiration
Flexibility	Integrity
Flow	Intelligence
Focus	Introversion
Freedom	Intuition
Friendliness	Inventiveness
Fun	Joy
Generosity	Kindness
Grace	Knowledge
Gratitude	Leadership
Growth	Learning
Guidance	Logic
Happiness	Love
Harmony	Loyalty
Health	Making a difference
Heroism	Mindfulness
Honesty	Modesty
Honor	Motivation
Hopefulness	Open-mindedness
Hospitality	Optimism
Humility	Organization
Humor	Originality
Imagination	Passion
Impact	Peace
Independence	Perceptiveness
Inquisitiveness	Perfection
Insightfulness	Perseverance

My Core Values

Philanthropy	Spirituality
Playfulness	Spontaneity
Pleasure	Stability
Power	Stillness
Practicality	Strength
Precision	Structure
Preparedness	Success
Professionalism	Support
Prosperity	Sympathy
Purity	Teamwork
Realism	Thankfulness
Recognition	Thoughtfulness
Recreation	Trust
Reflection	Trustworthiness
Relaxation	Truth
Resilience	Understanding
Resourcefulness	Uniqueness
Respect	Virtue
Satisfaction	Vision
Self-control	Willingness
Selflessness	Wisdom
Self-reliance	Wonder
Sensitivity	
Serenity	
Service	
Simplicity	
Sincerity	
Solitude	

My Top 30 Values

1. _____
2. _____
3. _____
4. _____
5. _____
6. _____
7. _____
8. _____
9. _____
10. _____
11. _____
12. _____
13. _____
14. _____
15. _____
16. _____
17. _____
18. _____
19. _____
20. _____
21. _____
22. _____
23. _____
24. _____
25. _____
26. _____
27. _____
28. _____
29. _____
30. _____

My Top 10 Values

1. _____

2. _____

3. _____

4. _____

5. _____

6. _____

7. _____

8. _____

9. _____

10. _____

My Top 10 Values,
ranked in order of importance

1. _____

2. _____

3. _____

4. _____

5. _____

6. _____

7. _____

8. _____

9. _____

10. _____

The Power of Music

Music is a powerful tool for so many reasons. We are attracted to music for its vibrational components, the emotional connection, and its instant affect on our mood. The energetic effects of music are supported by both research and common experience. This exercise is an opportunity to transform your daily radio time into self-love practice time.

As I was going through my divorce, the plethora of love songs on the radio used to aggravate me. It elicited my pity party of sadness, loneliness, and jealously. When I became aware that I needed to find a way to fall in love with myself, I began to listen to those songs in a different way.

I began by imagining that God (the Universe, Source, or whatever higher power resonates with you) was singing to me. I know how deeply and intensely I love my children, so it wasn't such a stretch to believe that the Universe could hold me in the same regard.

You can also listen to see if the song is a fit for how you feel about your kids. Some songs also work well to remind you of how your kids feel about you. The point is to begin to listen with a new perspective, and to use the opportunity to practice your new self-love messages.

From there, I moved toward internalizing. At first, I was a long way from being able to sing love songs to myself or my inner child. I simply didn't feel good enough about myself to do that with any sincerity. With practice, however, it became easier and easier to use the songs as an opportunity to love myself.

I invite you to listen for opportunities to shower love on yourself. Really listen to the love songs and discern truth for yourself. But realize that not all songs ring true for everybody. This is an exercise in trying on what someone else believes, and determining whether it's true for you. I am not suggesting that just because you hear something in a song, you should internalize it. Maintain your personal power and seize the opportunity to nurture your self-love.

Affirmations and Mirror Work

This exercise can serve as a litmus test of how you are truly feeling about yourself. When I suggest the idea of looking into your own eyes and saying "I love you," your immediate reaction reveals your current feelings about yourself. Like all growth and expansion, regular practice is the key. Your personal awareness plays a large role here.

Start with this. Grab your journal (or a piece of paper) and think about this exercise. Imagine staring into your own eyes in the mirror and saying, "I love you." Take a few minutes and write about the emotions this exercise stirs up for you. Are you nervous? Excited? Rebellious (i.e., think this exercise is stupid, won't work, etc.)? Sad? Whatever is coming up for you, write down these private thoughts. You don't need to share them with anyone, just get real with yourself. If it is very difficult for you to proclaim your love to yourself, use the information as a starting place on your self-love journey.

As you discover your feelings around this exercise, use the opportunity to renew your vow to yourself (see Chapter Two). If you seek to fall completely and totally in love with yourself, you'll need to take some action. This exercise is a good starting point.

Once you've discovered your initial reaction to the exercise, see how it feels to do it. Look into your own eyes. "I love you." Continue to practice this exercise every day or even several times a day until it feels good and true. When you are getting ready in the morning, styling your hair, or applying make-up, pay attention to the messages you are sending yourself. Are they messages of love and beauty? Or are they messages of wrinkles, blemishes, and perceived flaws?

Here's a guide: Whatever it is you are thinking, would you say it to your best friend? "Gee, Jennifer, your wrinkles are really deep and ugly. Don't know why you bother with make-up." Or, "Wow! You are one frumpy lady!" We realize how ridiculous it would be to say these things to anyone else, yet we continue to abuse ourselves with these negative messages.

The objective of mirror work is to begin to see yourself with the beauty, love, and joy with which you see others. You have an innate ability to see the beauty in the people you love, and it is absolutely time to look for and appreciate that beauty within yourself.

As you practice this exercise, expand it. Look for the beauty in your own eyes, in your own face. Declare your love for yourself in fun and joyful ways. Greet yourself with a positive statement such as, "Good morning, Gorgeous Lady! I love you so much!" It may feel insane right now, but with practice and commitment, these affirmations can help you shift your thoughts and move in the direction of falling completely and totally in love with yourself!

Dating Yourself

Many relationship experts recommend setting up a date night with your partner to ensure continued connection and bonding. The basic philosophy is "what we focus on expands" (see Chapter One, Perspective), and so if we invest specific energy into our relationships, we create a behavioral pattern that nurtures that relationship.

Your blooming relationship with yourself is no different.

I invite you to create a date night (or morning, or weekend) on a regular, scheduled basis. This is a time set aside for you to hang out with you. Again, if the very idea of this exercise freaks you out, use that information to become more aware of your thoughts about yourself. Get real with yourself and actively move toward changing the negative perception into self-honoring and self-celebration.

Use your date time to do a self-love exercise, read, journal, tune into nature, explore a museum, meditate, or whatever makes you feel cared for and loved. Make a commitment to the journey of discovering and loving yourself. You deserve the gift of your own love and attention.

Journaling

The process of journaling is incredibly powerful for a number of reasons.

- ◆ It gives you an earmark of your current position so you can see how far you've come.
- ◆ It allows you to explore your innermost thoughts and feelings in an honest and authentic manner.
- ◆ It helps you to straighten out stray thoughts.
- ◆ If you have a lot going on in your head, the process of journaling allows you to pay attention to each thought individually, write it down, and move on to the next thought. The simple acknowledgment of the thought can help quiet the mind.

Journaling also provides an opportunity for you to tap into your inner knowledge and seek guidance from within yourself. You know what is best for you. You have an inner voice that is continuously looking out for your best interest. Writing can help you get in touch with that inner voice and find clarity.

If you start a journaling practice, use it as an exercise in self-exploration and self-love. Remember to be gentle with yourself. Allow the practice to teach you about yourself and show you what you would like to create next in your life.

Taking the Vow (again and again)

Create your own version of the self-love vow (Chapter Two). Make a promise to value and take care of yourself. You may even want to print it and create a wall hanging or note card so that you can put it somewhere that will remind you of this commitment to yourself. You can download a template on www.ilovememom.com.

You can use the suggested vow on pages 46 and 47 as a starting point, and you may want to customize it with your personality and specific desires.

Consider including thoughts about:

- Releasing guilt.
- Falling completely and totally in love with yourself and your inner child.
- Consciously honoring your needs, and putting them at the top of your priority list.

- ♦ Trusting that others have the ability to take care of themselves.
- ♦ Operating from love and joy.
- ♦ Recommitting to this vow as often as necessary.

Once you've written out your vow, continue to read and absorb the message and celebrate the progress you are making!

I AM
SpeciAl.
And
So ARE You.

The journey of 1000 miles begins with one step. Awareness is the perfect first step. Now that you have some new awareness about the importance of your relationship with yourself, it is my sincere hope that you will invest in that relationship. You deserve all the happiness that life has to offer, and in my experience, true happiness is born from self-love.

You can see the potential in your children. And your love for them illustrates the capacity for love that we all have. Accepting that love from yourself is a tremendous gift—not only to yourself, but also to your children, and to the world. We can positively change how we perceive our experiences, and we can make a difference in how our children travel through life.

I am so grateful to have had the opportunity to share these ideas with you. I hope that you will revisit them anytime you forget how powerful, beautiful, and awesome you truly are!

About the Author

Following a complete life implosion in 2008, Jill leaned into her rebellious spirit and set out on an adventure of personal development, service, and life experiments. Along the way, Jill studied and explored behavioral psychology, parenting, leadership, coaching, metaphysics, emotions, energy, spiritual connections, relationships, business, science, and more. With a unique ability to translate the complex to the obvious, Jill helps people identify their power and responsibility in any story while building confidence, self-awareness, and joy. Jill works with clients that want to create and experience extraordinary lives. She lives near Milwaukee, WI with her two children.